'Twas the Season of Lent

Devotions and Stories for the Lenten and Easter Seasons

ZONDERKIDZ

'Twas the Season of Lent
Copyright © 2024 by Glenys Nellist
Illustrations © 2024 by Elena Selivanova

Requests for information should be addressed to:
Zonderkidz, 3900 Sparks Dr. SE, Grand Rapids, Michigan 49546

Hardcover ISBN 978-0-310-13937-9
Ebook ISBN 978-0-310-13938-6

All Scripture quotations, unless otherwise indicated, are taken from The Holy Bible, *New International Version®, NIV®.* Copyright © 1973, 1978, 1984, 2011 by Biblica, Inc.® Used by permission. All rights reserved worldwide.

Art direction and design: Cindy Davis

Printed in Malaysia

24 25 26 27 28 29 30 /IMG/ 20 19 18 17 16 15 14 13 12 11 10 9 8 7 6 5 4 3 2 1

Written by Glenys Nellist
Illustrated by Elena Selivanova

THE MISSION OF JESUS

'Twas the season of Lent, when for forty whole days
God's people were trying to think of new ways
To be more like Jesus—to love, care, and give—
In hopes that they'd choose the right way to live.

On this journey through Lent they were hoping to find
How to forgive, to pray, and be kind.
To think less of themselves, how to put others first,
To help heal the world of its sorrows and hurts.

But the story of Lent began long, long ago …
In a dry, dusty desert where no flowers grow.
For forty long days and forty long nights
Jesus listened to God and chose what was right.

DAY ONE

Welcoming Lent

Welcome to the holy season of Lent. Do you know what Lent means? Lent is the time when we get ready for Easter. Lent is related to the word springtime. Look outside your window. Maybe it doesn't look like spring yet. Perhaps the ground is covered with a white blanket of snow; the skies above might be gray and the trees may be bare. That's because springtime is a waiting time. The bulbs planted deep in the dark soil will be waking up soon. The buds on the trees are quietly waiting to burst into bloom. We know that all the earth is getting ready to grow and change.

Lent is a waiting time too. For forty days we wait for Easter to come. And as we wait, we get ready—

to grow and change,

to listen to God,

to ask questions,

to think about the choices we make,

to try to put God first.

For the next forty days, we will journey through Lent together. We'll begin in a dry, dusty desert and end in a hope-filled garden. As we travel, we'll hear the stories of Jesus; we'll find out what Jesus said about living well and loving others; about what is important and who is important. And as we turn the pages, God will be with us on this journey—helping us to grow, helping us to change, helping us to get ready for Easter.

Welcome to Lent.

Prayer
Dear God, thank you for this book we hold.
Thank you for being with us as we journey through Lent together.

DAY TWO

Forty Days and Forty Nights
Mark 1:9–13

I t was hot and quiet and still in the desert. Jesus was thirsty. He closed his eyes and thought about the day before, when his friend, John, had plunged him under the cold, clear waters of the River Jordan. How glorious it had felt to be baptized! Jesus remembered seeing the clouds part above his head, as if the gates of heaven had opened to let God speak nine wonderful words that Jesus would never, ever forget:

You are my son. I am pleased with you.

Jesus opened his eyes and smiled. He knew who he was. He was God's own son. And God was pleased with him.

Jesus stayed in the desert for forty long days and forty long nights.

> Nothing to eat.
> Nothing to drink.
> Listening to God.
> Trying to think.

Under the blazing hot sun by day and the light of the silver moon by night, Jesus talked to God.

What do you want me to do?

And whenever he heard a voice that tempted him to think about himself, Jesus closed his eyes and thought about God instead.

When the forty days were over, Jesus knew what God wanted him to do. He stood up, wrapped his cloak around himself, and set out for the synagogue in Nazareth, leaving a trail of footprints behind him in the sand.

Prayer
Dear God, during these next forty days, help us find time to listen to you.
Help us to think about what you want us to do.

DAY THREE

Good News

Luke 4:16–22

It was so quiet in the synagogue in Nazareth you could have heard a cricket cough. No one moved. No one spoke. Everyone stood, looking at Jesus, as he walked to the front, took hold of the scroll, unrolled it slowly, and began to read the ancient words written by the prophet Isaiah many, many years before …

God's Spirit is upon me.
I've heard God's gentle call,
To reach out to the poor,
To bring Good News to all.
I'm here to help the lonely,
To set the prisoners free,
To spread the love of God,
And help the blind to see.

Jesus sat down. Still, no one moved. No one spoke. They didn't know what to say. They weren't sure if they wanted to share what they had with the poor. And how could they help the lonely? Would that mean they would have to spend time with people they didn't know or like? The people listening began to mutter and mumble. They shook their heads. They didn't really want to change.

Jesus looked through the doors of the synagogue to where the hills of Galilee seemed to beckon to him, and beyond those hills lay the blue waters of the lake. Jesus knew where to find people who were ready to change. He left the synagogue behind and set out for the beach.

Prayer

Thank you, God, for the Good News that Jesus brought to all those who were poor or
hungry or lonely. Help us to think about how we can bring good news to others this Lent.

DAY FOUR

Follow Me

Matthew 4:18–22

On the shores of Lake Galilee four fishermen sat cleaning their nets in the early morning sun. For as long as they could remember, every day had been the same.

Simon Peter, Andrew, James, and John would get up early each morning, head down to the beach, climb into their fishing boats, sail into deep waters, and throw their nets overboard to catch fish. When their nets were full, they would return to shore, load the fish into baskets, and then clean their nets, ready to begin all over again the next morning.

But *this* morning was different.

A man named Jesus, who they'd never met before, walked toward them on the beach, called their names, and said just two simple words:

Follow me.

And they did.

We don't know if those four fishermen had heard of Jesus before that day. We don't know how they felt when Jesus called them. We don't know if they asked any questions. But what we do know is that they said yes. Simon Peter, Andrew, James, and John left everything behind. They left their nets, their fish, their boats, and their jobs, to follow Jesus.

Over the next few days, eight other men joined Jesus. Those twelve men became Jesus's first disciples and soon, many others, including women, would follow Jesus too. Together, those first disciples and followers of Jesus would change the world.

Prayer
Thank you, God, for those first men and women who said yes to Jesus and followed him.
Help us to think carefully about what it would mean for us to follow Jesus.

DAY FIVE

How to Be Happy

Matthew 6:26–29

Those first twelve disciples who followed Jesus were ordinary men. Most of them were fishermen, and one was a tax collector. They knew a lot about how to catch fish, how to mend a boat, or how to save money. But they didn't know anything about God, or heaven, or how to pray. And so, in those early days, Jesus set about teaching them all these important things.

Very often, he would sit with them on a hillside overlooking Lake Galilee. Along with crowds of other people, Jesus would tell them stories and teach them everything he knew about God.

"Who wants to be happy?" Jesus asked one day. Everyone nodded and sat up, carefully waiting to hear what Jesus would say next.

"Happiness doesn't come from having lots of money or owning a big home," said Jesus. "Happiness comes from knowing what God wants you to do."

The disciples looked puzzled.

"How do we find out what God wants us to do?" they asked.

Jesus smiled. He was a good teacher. But he didn't have any pictures to show or books to read aloud. He didn't have a whiteboard or markers or a computer screen. Instead, Jesus told stories about all the ordinary things that could be seen around them on that Galilean hillside … like the birds flying in the air, the lilies nodding in the fields, the sheep grazing in the meadow, or the farmers sowing seeds. Jesus used all these things to teach the disciples. They were ready to learn about God and what God wanted them to do. Their journey was just beginning.

Prayer

Thank you, God, for the stories Jesus told. Help us to be good listeners, just like those first disciples.

DAY SIX

Putting God First
Matthew 6:25–34

esus sat with his twelve disciples and a crowd of listeners on the hillside overlooking Lake Galilee. Down below, the fishing boats the disciples had left behind bobbed up and down on the sunlit waves as seagulls dipped and dived over the water.

"Look at the birds of the air," said Jesus. "Do you think those birds worry about their life, about what they eat or what they drink?" All the people listening shook their heads.

"That's right," said Jesus. "And God doesn't want you to worry about your life either."

"Or look at the flowers in the fields," said Jesus. The people looked over at the lovely colorful lilies as they nodded and danced in the wind. "Do you think they worry about how they look?" All the people listening shook their heads.

"That's right," said Jesus. "And God doesn't want you to worry about how you look either."

"Now if God takes such good care of the birds in the air and the lilies in the fields, don't you think God will take much better care of you?" This time, all the people listening nodded their heads.

"Try to put God first," said Jesus. "And God will take care of everything you need."

A peace settled on the hillside as everyone thought about Jesus's words.

God was holding them.

Prayer
Thank you, God, for holding us through this Lenten season.
Help us as we figure out how to put you first.

Let Your Light Shine

Matthew 5:14–16; 43–46

t was getting late on the hillside above Lake Galilee. The sun had sunk down low over the hills and the early evening shadows were creeping over the grass. But the crowd that had gathered to listen to Jesus was still listening to his words as he taught his disciples.

"Did you know," said Jesus, "that God's great love for you is longer than the longest river, higher than the tallest mountain, and deeper than the deepest ocean? God's love for you will last forever and ever. And because everyone is included in God's great love, one of the most important things God wants you to do is to share that love with others. But here's the thing—don't just love your friends or your families—anyone can do that! You must try hard to love your enemies too. Love the people you find hard to love, love the ones you don't like, pray for them, and be kind to them."

As the evening shadows fell, Jesus lit a torch and held it up so the flames flickered in the darkness.

"Look at this flame," said Jesus. "Everyone can see it as it burns. It lights up everything around it. Love is like that. Love is like a light that burns brightly in the darkness. When you love others, people everywhere can see it. When your love for others is strong, it will bring light and hope and joy to everyone around you. Love strong, love long! Let your love shine like a light in this dark world."

All the people on the hillside watched that flame as it flickered and danced in the darkness. In their hearts, they wanted to love like that. Jesus was teaching them how.

Prayer
Dear God, help us to think carefully about how to let the light of your love shine in our lives.

DAY EIGHT

Let the Children Come

Matthew 19:13–15

 f you had been on that hillside in Galilee when Jesus and his disciples were gathered there one day, you might have seen some moms coming with their children. Some of the children ran ahead, some held their mom's hand, and the littlest ones were carried. You might have heard them laughing or shouting with excitement or clapping their hands. The children had heard about this wonderful new teacher called Jesus and they wanted to meet him for themselves.

But the disciples did something strange. Instead of welcoming the children, the disciples tried to send them away. Perhaps they thought Jesus was too busy to meet the children. Or perhaps they thought the children were too young to understand what Jesus said. But the disciples were wrong. As soon as Jesus saw what was happening, he stopped the disciples and said, "Let the children come to me."

So they did.

The children ran to Jesus, jumped on his lap, laughed with him, and listened to him.

Perhaps the disciples remembered then what Jesus had said about God's great love, and how it included everyone, no matter how old or young, no matter what clothes they wore, where they lived, or the color of their skin. God's great love was (and still is) for all.

God's great love included the children.

And God's great love includes you.

Prayer

*Thank you, God, that in your great love there
is room for everyone—including us.*

DAY NINE

Questions for Jesus
John 3:1–21

One night a man named Nicodemus knocked on Jesus's door. Nicodemus was a follower of God, and a great teacher himself. He knew all God's laws that had been written down hundreds of years before and he did his best to follow them. But he was curious about who Jesus was and he had lots of questions for him.

Who are you? Nicodemus wanted to know. Why are you here?

But when Jesus answered, his words were full of mystery, deep meaning, and wonder.

If you want to see God's Kingdom, you might have to change.

The Holy Spirit is invisible, but it's real, just like the wind.

Light has come into the world.

What must Nicodemus have thought about Jesus's answers? Did he think about them when he finally got home that night? Jesus hadn't really answered his questions in a way that Nicodemus could understand. Nicodemus must have gone to bed still puzzling over who Jesus was and trying to work out why Jesus came.

Lent is a good time for us to ask questions too. We can think deeply about who Jesus is, why he came, and what it is that God wants us to do with our everyday lives. As we ponder those things, God will be with us as we try to make meaning out of mystery, just like God was with Nicodemus.

Prayer
Thank you, God, that we can ask questions as we try to
learn more about who Jesus is and why he came.

DAY TEN

Our Journey Through Lent

ver since Jesus invited those first disciple to join him on an exciting new journey, people all over the world have tried to find ways to journey with Jesus too. Sometimes, journeying with Jesus might be hard. Even though it was an exciting time for those early followers, it wasn't always easy to understand everything Jesus said, and it was hard to find out what God wanted them to do. Jesus was a great teacher, but the disciples still had to listen well, ask questions, learn how to pray, try to find ways to put God first in their lives, and love others (even the ones they found it hard to love).

But the wonderful thing about Jesus was that he didn't just talk about loving God and loving others—Jesus showed them how. Everywhere Jesus went, he listened to everyone who came to him, helped those who needed help, prayed for them, and taught them everything he knew about God.

Our journey through Lent might be a bit like the journey those disciples took—it might be hard to understand what Jesus says and hard to find out what God wants us to do. But as we journey, we can know that God is with us …

helping us to listen,
welcoming our questions,
listening as we pray,
showing us how to love others,
and helping us find ways to put God first.

And even if we don't know it, we will be growing closer to Jesus, and changing as God works in our lives.

Prayer
Thank you, God, that you are at work in our lives even when we don't know it.

THE MESSAGE OF JESUS

Then Jesus set out and found a good team
Of women and men who shared God's great dream.
And out on the hillside and by the lakeshore
His followers listened, eager for more.

He taught them to love, he taught them to pray,
He told them that God was with them each day.
And the calm in his voice, the words that he said,
Soon let listeners know—they had nothing to dread.

DAY ELEVEN

Fasting

Matthew 6:16–18

D o you remember when Jesus went into the desert for forty days and forty nights?

Nothing to eat.
Nothing to drink.
Listening to God.
Trying to think.

Forty days and forty nights is a long time to go without food and drink! Only the Son of God could do that! But during Lent, many people **do** try to give up certain foods or meals, so that they can spend more time listening to God. It gives them a chance to think carefully about what God wants them to do. It is called *fasting*.

"But when you fast," Jesus told his followers, "don't do it in a loud way. Don't show off in front of others. Fast quietly. God can see, and God knows your heart."

Sometimes, instead of giving something up, people choose to *add* something to their day. They might read the Bible more, try harder to pray, or find ways to help others. When they do those things, they feel closer to Jesus.

Whatever you decide to do during Lent—whether you fast, try to give something up, or add something to your day, these are all wonderful ways to help you think more about God.

Prayer
Dear God, help us to think carefully about what we can give up,
or add, so that we can think more about you this Lent.

DAY TWELVE

How to Pray

Matthew 6:5–8

an you guess what Jesus did whenever he felt sad or afraid or he had a big decision to make? That's right—he prayed. Very often, Jesus would get up early in the morning while it was still dark and go, all by himself, into the hills to pray. We don't know many of the words Jesus said, but we do know that he spent time listening as well as talking to God.

When the disciples asked Jesus to teach them how to pray, Jesus told them, "Your prayers don't need to be loud. Pray quietly. God is listening. Your prayers don't need to be long. Pray simply. After all, God already knows everything you need."

If Jesus were here today, he would tell us the same thing he told his disciples:

> *Pray quietly.*
> *Pray simply.*

Today Jesus would encourage us to find our own ways to pray, ways that feel comfortable to us—whether we put our hands together and close our eyes, whether we pray when we're still or active, whether we're together or alone, or it's bedtime or mealtime, whether we say our prayers out loud or in the quietness of our hearts. Wherever we are, whatever we're doing, God is with us.

And God, who already knows all our needs, is listening.

Prayer

Thank you, God, that we can pray to you in many different ways.
Help us remember that however or wherever we pray, you are always listening.

DAY THIRTEEN

What to Pray

Matthew 6:9–13

Over two thousand years ago, Jesus sat with his disciples and taught them a very simple but powerful prayer that we know today as *The Lord's Prayer*.

If Jesus were teaching us this prayer today, he might use words like this:

Our God, who lives in heaven,

May your name be holy.

May your good kingdom come to all the earth,

And may what you want always be done.

Thank you for giving us the food we need each day.

Forgive us when we do things wrong,

And give us the strength to forgive others.

Lead us down a good path, one that leads to you,

So that we make the right choices.

Because this world and everything in it—

All of it—belongs to you.

Amen.

When you say those ancient words, pause for a moment and think about how you are connected to the first disciples who heard Jesus say them over two thousand years ago. Those followers taught this prayer to their children, who passed it on to their own children, and then their grandchildren, until one day, someone wrote those ancient words down.

Today, those same words have been translated into over 1,800 languages and are either spoken aloud or prayed in silence each day by millions of Christians all around the world.

When you say *The Lord's Prayer* you are connected to a huge worldwide family of people who follow Jesus.

That is the power of prayer.

Prayer

Thank you, God, for the prayer that Jesus taught his disciples so long ago.
Thank you for the person who wrote them down, so that we can still say them today.

DAY FOURTEEN

What's Important?

Matthew 6:19–21

Imagine that one day you found a treasure box someone had carefully hidden away. What would you expect to find if you peeped inside? Perhaps that treasure box contains money, or jewels, precious coins, or trinkets made of silver and gold.

A treasure box usually holds things that are important to the person who owns it. But suppose that treasure box got lost or stolen … or what if the precious jewels got rusty? Then what good would that treasure be?

Jesus talked about a different kind of treasure that we can store away. Can you imagine a treasure box that's invisible, one that's kept safely for you in heaven?

A treasure box like that might be full of all the kind things you've ever said, all the good things you've ever done, and all the love you've shared with others. Wouldn't that be a wonderful treasure box? No one could ever steal those things and that kind of treasure would last forever.

Jesus told his followers, "Don't worry about storing treasures on earth, instead, store up treasures in heaven. Those kinds of treasures will last forever."

And that's what's important.

Prayer

Dear God, help us to think carefully about the
kind of treasures we should store up during Lent.

DAY FIFTEEN

Giving

Mark 12:41–44

Jesus was sitting in the temple courtyard one day, watching people as they put their money in the big offering box. Loud trumpets announced the arrival of a man dressed in fine robes, fancy sandals, and a big expensive hat. He paraded up to the offering box carrying a huge bag filled to the brim with shiny gold coins. Everyone watched as he threw in several coins. They clattered loudly as they fell into the box. Then the man strode away.

Next, there came a poor widow in bare feet who crept quietly up to the box. Only Jesus watched as she emptied her purse and put in all she had. It was just two tiny copper coins. They fell without a sound into the offering box. Then the woman crept away.

"You might think," said Jesus to his disciples, "that the man gave more than the woman, but you'd be wrong. That woman gave from her huge, generous heart. She gave all she had. Give quietly, give from the heart, and always, always give what you can."

Prayer
Dear God, help us to be generous givers
with generous hearts this Lent.

DAY SIXTEEN

Making Good Choices
Luke 10:25–37

ne day Jesus told a story about a man who had been attacked by robbers. He was lying beside the road when a priest came walking by. But instead of helping, the priest chose to cross over to the other side of the road.

Soon a priest's assistant came walking by. But instead of helping, the priest's assistant chose to cross over to the other side of the road.

Soon a traveler from another town came walking by. But instead of crossing over to the other side of the road, the traveler helped the man to his feet, took him to an inn, and paid the innkeeper to take good care of him.

"Who do you think made the right choice in that story?" Jesus asked.

"The man who helped," came the reply.

"Then you go into the world and make good choices too," said Jesus. "Be ready to help your neighbor, whoever they are, however you can, and wherever you can."

Prayer
God, help us to make good choices, not just during these forty days, but every day.
Help us to be ready to help our neighbors, whoever they are, however we can, and wherever we can.

DAY SEVENTEEN

Spring Cleaning

Luke 15:8–10

Have you ever noticed how some people like to 'spring clean' their homes at this time of year? Some folks get busy clearing all the clutter from their closets. They might wash their windows, rearrange furniture, and throw garbage away. For many people, spring is a good time to make a fresh start. If you've ever cleaned your room up, you probably felt good about how it looked after.

There was a woman like that in the Bible too. She was in a story Jesus told. But she wasn't just spring cleaning her home—she was searching for a very important silver coin she'd lost.

The woman lit a lamp and used it to search under the table, the bed, the chair, and the rug. She scoured every corner and hunted through every cupboard. Then she moved all the furniture and swept the floor with a broom—until finally, she found her precious coin.

She was so overjoyed that she ran out into the streets and shouted to her neighbors, "Rejoice with me! I have found my lost coin!"

Jesus said that God rejoices like that whenever any of us come closer to God. Lent is a great time to do that. It's a good time to 'spring clean' our lives—to think carefully about how we use our time, to get rid of any 'clutter' that gets in the way of us spending time with God, and to make a fresh start through praying, reading the Bible more, or helping others.

And just like we feel good when we've cleaned up our rooms, we'll feel good about how we're living.

Prayer
Dear God, help us to use this Lenten time to 'spring clean' our lives.

DAY EIGHTEEN

Growing

Matthew 13:1–9

One day Jesus stood in a fishing boat on the edge of Lake Galilee and told a story about a farmer who went out to sow some seeds.

Some of the seeds fell on the path, where the birds came and ate them up. Some fell on rocky, hard ground, where they were scorched by the hot sun. Still others fell among thorns that wrapped around the shoots and stopped them from growing.

But some of that seed fell on good, deep soil, where the roots took hold. Those seeds grew into plants that were tall and lovely and strong.

All the people on the beach listened carefully, but Jesus's words were hard to understand.

"What does that story mean?" the disciples asked Jesus later. And Jesus told them, "Close your eyes. Imagine all those seeds. Imagine how the farmer feels about each one. Now suppose God is the farmer, sowing seeds of love in your hearts. Is your heart a place where love can grow?"

And then the disciples knew. They needed to take care of their hearts like a garden, so those seeds of love could grow.

Prayer
Help me, God, to keep growing in your love.

DAY NINETEEN

Finding Rest

Matthew 11:28–29

hen Jesus taught his followers on that hillside or by the lakeshore in Galilee, he knew they might sometimes feel anxious about the words he said. He knew they might sometimes feel like they weren't good enough to please God. But when those followers thought things like:

I'm not good enough …
I don't know how to put God first …
I don't always make the right choices …
I'm not a good follower …

Jesus whispered words of love into their hearts. Jesus just kept encouraging them and reassuring them that God loved them *no matter what*. Most importantly, Jesus told them,

"Come to me, whenever you're tired, and I will give you rest."

If you're feeling anxious this Lent (or ANY time), and you wonder if you're good enough for God, or doing enough for God, hear Jesus whisper those same words to you—

"God loves you just as you are. Come to me, and I will give you rest."

Take a walk outside, do something fun, read a book, make cookies, laugh—God is with you.

Prayer
Dear God, if ever I'm finding things hard this Lent (or any other time), help me remember that you love me no matter what and you are always, always with me.

DAY TWENTY

Halfway Through Lent

e are now halfway through our Lenten journey together. It's a good time to pause, to think about what we've read, and look forward to what is to come as we continue our journey toward Easter.

Look outside your window, like you did when you first began reading this book. Is it still covered in snow where you are? Are the branches on the trees still bare? Even if they are, do you know what you'd see if you could peep under the dark, cold earth? You'd see bulbs and roots and shoots, getting ready to push their way out of the ground.

And if you could take a very close look at those bare tree branches, you might just see tiny tufts of green, heralding the arrival of spring as new buds get ready to appear.

In many ways, our slow journey through Lent is like that too. We might not be able to see our faith in Jesus growing. We might think nothing is happening in our lives. But with every story we read and every prayer we say, with every kind deed we do and every right choice we make; whatever we've given up this Lent or whatever we've added to our day, all those things are helping us think more about God and what God wants us to do.

Together, we are growing, learning how to put God first, praying more, and loving more. And even though we're not gathered on that hillside in Galilee, or sitting on the shore of the lake with Jesus, we are all disciples and followers of Jesus, listening to his words, journeying together toward Easter.

Prayer
Dear God, thank you for what we are learning together this Lent.
Be with us as we begin the second half of our journey toward Easter.

25

THE MINISTRY OF JESUS

For those who were lonely, left out, or in pain,
It was Jesus who saw them and called them by name.
He brought hope to ALL with words that were true
To Martha and Mary and Zacchaeus too.

Whether young or old, or tiny or tall,
None of that mattered to Jesus at all.
Friend to the friendless, the sad or the scared,
Everyone loved the Good News Jesus shared.

DAY TWENTY-ONE

Ready to Change
Luke 19:1–10

 acchaeus, the tax collector, sat high in the sycamore tree, waiting for Jesus to pass by. Since he was too short to see over the heads of the crowd gathered in the street below, it would be a great view. Like everyone else, Zacchaeus was curious about the new teacher in town. Who was this man who could make sick people well, and who taught about loving others?

As Zacchaeus waited, he thought about all the money he'd collected in the huge purse hidden under his bed. It was true he'd taken a bit more than he should from his neighbors, but he hadn't cheated them *that* much.

Suddenly Zacchaeus heard cheering coming from the street and peered through the leaves to see Jesus walking down the road with his twelve disciples. But Zacchaeus couldn't help being disappointed. This man looked like any other man. There was nothing special about him.

As soon as he leaves, I'll go home, Zacchaeus thought. But Jesus didn't leave. He stopped, looked right up through the branches, and spoke to Zacchaeus.

"Zacchaeus, come down. I want to eat with you."

Zacchaeus nearly fell out of the tree. The crowd was as shocked as he was. Why did Jesus want to talk with *him*? Didn't Jesus know he was a cheater? But there was something in the way this man spoke that made Zacchaeus want to learn more.

The people who lived in Jericho never knew what Jesus said to Zacchaeus. All they knew was that the very next day, Zacchaeus was running through the streets of Jericho with his huge purse, giving back all the money he'd taken and more besides, until he had almost no money left.

Zacchaeus had changed. Money wasn't important to him anymore. Love was.

Prayer
Thank you, God, that when we listen to Jesus, we can change so that love becomes the most important thing.

DAY TWENTY-TWO

Choosing to Share

John 6:1–13

ver 5,000 tummies were rumbling on the hillside in Galilee. The huge crowd that had gathered to hear Jesus teach was hungry. The sun was setting. There were no shops in sight. Where would they get dinner?

The little boy whose mom had packed a lovely picnic for him that very morning was the only one who wasn't worried. He peeped into his basket where the beady eyes of two small fish peeped back, and the smell of five little loaves wafted out.

"Is there anyone here who brought any food they will share?" the little boy heard the disciples ask.

The boy only hesitated for a moment before raising his hand. He knew there wasn't enough food for everyone in his basket, but he would gladly give what he had to Jesus.

Jesus smiled, lifted the basket, thanked God, then had everyone sit down as he began to break the bread. Under the setting sun, that huge crowd shared dinner together. No one understood how it happened. The bread just kept appearing. The fish just kept appearing, until all those tummies were full.

It was a miracle only Jesus could do. But it began with a little boy who was ready to share.

Prayer
Dear God, help us remember that sometimes,
miracles can begin with us.

DAY TWENTY-THREE

The Woman at the Well

John 4:1–42

The Samaritan woman watched the bucket as she lowered it deep into the well. With every turn of the handle, she thought about her life and how empty it was.

Get up. Make breakfast. Clean the house. Trudge to the well. Get water. Carry it back. Make dinner. Go to bed. Get up … She felt like her days had no purpose or meaning. But today was going to be different …

"Could you get me a drink of water?"

The woman turned around, shocked to see a man sitting close by. He was a Jew. She was a Samaritan. Why was he talking to her?

"Sir," she replied. "Why are you talking to me? You don't know me."

"But I do know you," said Jesus softly. "I know you are lonely. I know you are looking for love. And I also know that God's love for you is deeper than this well."

The woman was confused. "I know that when Jesus comes, he will explain all that to us," she replied.

Jesus looked into her eyes and said, "I am He."

Suddenly, the woman knew it was true. She had met the One who could bring meaning and hope to her life! She jumped up, ran into town, and told the news to everyone she met. Jesus stayed in that town for three days, until everyone there knew about God's love too.

And each day after that, the woman's routine was different.

Get up. Pray. Do a good deed. Smile. Help a neighbor. Sing. Tell someone about Jesus. Be thankful.

The woman's life wasn't empty anymore. It was filled with meaning and hope. And her heart was filled with peace.

Prayer
*Thank you, God, that when we know Jesus, our days can be filled
with meaning and hope, and our hearts can be filled with peace.*

DAY TWENTY-FOUR

Be Still

Mark 4:35–44

he little boat that carried Jesus and his disciples across Lake Galilee was in big trouble. The storm had come suddenly, without warning. Torrential rain pounded from the sky. Violent winds whipped across the water and flung huge waves in the air. In the little boat, the disciples were terrified and clung on for dear life.

"Where's Jesus?" cried Andrew. "We need him!"

But believe it or not, Jesus was fast asleep, snoozing with his head on a comfy pillow while the storm raged all around.

"Jesus, wake up!" the disciples cried as another huge wave rocked the boat.

Jesus stood up, held his hands out over the water, and said two little words:

Be still.

And just like that, the storm was stilled to a whisper. The waves went down. The rain stopped. The little boat rocked gently on calm waters.

The disciples looked at Jesus. Who was this man?

Prayer

Thank you, God, that even in the scariest of times, Jesus is with us. Help us during Lent to take time to be still and think about who Jesus really is.

DAY TWENTY-FIVE

Being a Good Friend

Mark 2:1–12

The mat that the four men carried their friend on was getting heavy. It swung from side to side as they hurried through the streets of Capernaum. The healer called Jesus was in town and teaching at Peter's house. If they could get their friend to Jesus, they knew he'd be able to walk again.

Their friend had always felt left out. But if anyone could change his life, Jesus could.

But as they rounded the corner, they stopped in dismay. There was no way they could get in Peter's house. It was so full that the crowd was spilling out of the doorway. How would they get inside?

But those four friends didn't turn back. They gripped the mat firmly, climbed the steps up to the roof, dug and clawed and hammered a hole, and then gently lowered their friend down, until he landed at Jesus's feet.

In less than five minutes, their friend, who hadn't walked for many years, was running through the streets of Capernaum, whooping and laughing and thanking God.

Not only had he found Jesus, but that man had the best friends ever. He would never feel left out again.

Prayer

Thank you, God, that you don't want anyone to be left out. Help us to be the very best friends we can be, not just during Lent, but beyond.

DAY TWENTY-SIX

Who's Important?

Mark 5:21–43

There was once a very important man who lived in Capernaum. His name was Jairus, and he was a leader in the synagogue. One day he came striding through the streets of the town and fell at Jesus's feet. "Jesus, my little daughter is dying. I know you can heal her. Please come—now!"

Jesus immediately began to follow the man, but he hadn't gone far when he felt someone touch the hem of his robe. Jesus stopped. "Who touched me?" he asked.

The disciples were confused. Jesus was surrounded by a huge crowd, pressing in on every side.

"Everyone is touching you," they said.

But Jesus looked down and saw a woman at his feet. She had been ill for twelve long years. She had no friends. No one wanted to be near her. She was an outcast.

"I'm so sorry," she said, as Jesus looked down at her. "I just wanted to get better. I knew if I could only touch your robe, I would be healed."

Jesus knelt down in front of her, lifted her chin, and looked deep into her eyes.

"My daughter," Jesus said softly, "you are healed."

And she was.

Jesus continued on to Jairus's house, where he healed his little girl too.

Jairus, his daughter, and the woman who needed healing—they were all equally important to Jesus.

Prayer
God, during this Lenten season, help us remember that whoever we meet, whoever we see, we are ALL equally important to you.

DAY TWENTY-SEVEN

Mary and Martha

Luke 10:38–42

t was an exciting day for Mary and Martha when Jesus arrived at their home. Martha wanted to cook a meal for him and scurried around the kitchen, getting everything ready. Mary wanted to listen to Jesus teaching and sat at his feet so that she wouldn't miss anything he said.

After a while Martha came out of the kitchen, went up to Jesus, and said, "Jesus, don't you care that my sister has left me to do all the work by myself? Tell her to help me!"

But Jesus smiled and kindly said, "Martha, Martha, you're so busy and upset and worried. Come and sit here too."

We don't know if Martha did what Jesus suggested. We don't know if Mary helped her sister later. What we do know is that Jesus cared about Martha, and whatever it was that upset her.

How wonderful to know that Jesus knows all our feelings and offers us a space at his feet where we can set our worries and our busyness aside.

Prayer
Dear God, help us, during the busyness of Lent,
to set aside time to be with you.

DAY TWENTY-EIGHT

Something Beautiful for Jesus

Matthew 26:6–13

 esus and his disciples were sitting around a table eating dinner one day when the door slowly opened, and Mary of Bethany came in. In her hands she carried an alabaster jar full of expensive perfume.

As everyone watched, she quietly went to Jesus, poured the fragrant oil over his feet, and began to dry them with her hair.

The men were outraged. "What a waste!" they cried.

But Jesus spoke up for Mary, just like he always did.

"That wasn't a waste. That was a wonderful, beautiful thing. What Mary did for me today will always be remembered."

And it was.

Prayer

Dear God, help me think about what beautiful things
I might be able to do for Jesus this Lent.

DAY TWENTY-NINE

Love for Everyone

Matthew 8:1–3

ave you heard of a skin disease called leprosy? In Bible times, many people had this disease. They were called lepers. There was no cure for leprosy, and because other people didn't want to catch it, lepers had to live alone. No one would touch them—except Jesus.

Jesus reached out in love, touched the lepers, and made them better.

And the wonderful thing about Jesus was that he reached out in love to *anyone* and *everyone*.

When the disciples thought he shouldn't spend time with children, Jesus did.

When others thought he shouldn't have a conversation with a Samaritan woman, Jesus did.

When the crowd thought he shouldn't make friends with Zacchaeus, Jesus did.

When men thought he shouldn't stand up for women, Jesus did.

When his followers thought he shouldn't touch the lepers, Jesus did.

Jesus reached out to heal, hold, and bring hope to *everyone*, no matter who they were, how old they were, what they'd done, or where they came from.

What a wonderful world it would be if all the followers of Jesus would do that too.

Prayer
Dear God, as followers of Jesus, help us have the courage to love like he did.

DAY THIRTY

The Mystery of Jesus

John 10:7, 11, 17–18

Did you know that one of the names Jesus used for himself was the *Good Shepherd?*

A day in the life of a shepherd in Galilee was a very busy one. A shepherd would know all his sheep and would take very good care of them. In the daytime, a shepherd would lead his sheep to find the best grass and the cleanest water. And when darkness fell, a shepherd would lead his sheep into the fold—a safe place surrounded by rocks or fences. If there was no gate, a good shepherd would lie down across the entrance to protect his sheep and become a gate for them.

"I am the Good Shepherd," Jesus said one day. "I am the gate. I lay down my life for the sheep. NO ONE takes my life from me. I lay it down by myself."

Jesus knew his time on earth was coming to an end. He knew he had lots of enemies who didn't like what he said about loving others and following God. Jesus knew that if he didn't stop talking about God, his enemies would try to kill him. But Jesus never stopped talking about God and showing people how to love others.

Jesus was like that good shepherd who would give up his own life to save his sheep.

We are Jesus's sheep and Jesus is our Good Shepherd.

That is the mystery of Jesus.

Prayer
Thank you, God, that Jesus loved others so much that he was ready to give his own life. Help us to think carefully about what that means to us.

THE MYSTERY OF JESUS

But sometimes when Jesus lay down in his bed,
Visions of danger danced round in his head.
His enemies came and they took him away.
And soon, Jesus died on a dark, lonely day.

The cave where they laid him was sealed with a stone.
The disciples and Mary were left all alone.
They couldn't believe that they'd lost their good friend,
But his story's not over—it wasn't the end!

DAY THIRTY-ONE

Ride into Jerusalem

Mark 11:8–10

Jesus couldn't help smiling as the little donkey carried him through the cheering crowds toward Jerusalem. He would try to enjoy this moment, even though he knew that his enemies were hiding behind those who waved palm branches to greet him.

The donkey trotted over colorful cloaks laid out like a carpet as the crowd shouted, *Hosanna! Blessed is he who comes in God's name!*

Jesus knew what *hosanna* meant.

Save us! Save us! they were pleading. Everyone thought that Jesus was going to be the new powerful king in town. Surely, he would fight the Romans who were in charge. Jesus would take much better care of them than the Romans did.

But Jesus didn't ride into Jerusalem to bring war. Jesus rode in to bring peace.

Jesus wouldn't carry weapons. Jesus would carry kindness.

Jesus wouldn't choose the way of the world. Jesus would choose the way of love.

Jesus stepped down from the donkey and turned toward Jerusalem.

He had just a few days left to show the world what love looked like.

Prayer
*Dear God, help us this Lent, whatever
we face, to try to choose the way of love.*

DAY THIRTY-TWO

What Love Looks Like

John 13:4–15

The twelve disciples were looking forward to a special dinner with Jesus. They knew he'd been busy getting everything ready for this night. Jesus had already found a quiet, upstairs room in Jerusalem where they wouldn't be disturbed. The disciples loved eating around a table with Jesus. It seemed like every time they did, Jesus told them special, mysterious, marvelous things.

Peter opened the door to the room, expecting to be met by the servant who would wash his dusty feet. But there was no servant. Instead, Jesus was kneeling down on the hard wooden floor next to a basin of water. He had a towel wrapped around his waist.

"Jesus!" Peter cried. "Where is the servant? Surely you aren't going to wash my feet!"

"I am," Jesus replied.

And taking Peter's dirty feet in his hands, he washed between every single one of Peter's toes, dried them, and then washed all the other disciples' feet too.

"Now you know what love looks like," said Jesus. "Love others. That is the way of love."

Prayer
Dear God, in this last week of Lent, show us how we can be a servant to others.

DAY THIRTY-THREE

The Way to Heaven

John 14:1–6

"on't let your hearts be troubled," said Jesus, as he looked around the table at his disciples. "And don't be afraid. Even when I leave you, there's nothing to worry about. I'm going somewhere special, but you will see me again. I'm going to come back. And one day you'll all be able to come to that special place too."

But the disciples were already worried. How could they not be afraid when Jesus said he was going to leave them?

"But where are you going?" they asked. "And how will we get there if we don't know the way?"

"Heaven is an easy place to find," said Jesus. "It's a place that's full of love. So if you keep loving others, you already know the way. Close your eyes. Imagine a huge, huge house with so many rooms that you can't count them all. That's my house. And there's room for everyone there."

The disciples still didn't understand, but when they closed their eyes and imagined that house, they felt better, because they could see themselves gathered there.

Prayer
Thank you, God, for heaven.

DAY THIRTY-FOUR

Remember Me

Luke 22:14–20

t was quiet in the upper room in Jerusalem.

In the middle of the table sat a huge pitcher of fresh wine. Next to it was a platter holding a lovely loaf of bread.

Jesus picked up the bread and broke it. The disciples watched as crumbs fell to the table. In turn, Jesus gave each of the disciples a piece of that broken bread.

"Whenever you eat bread," he said softly, "remember me."

Then he poured them each a drink of wine.

"Whenever you drink wine," he said softly, "remember me."

The disciples ate the bread. They drank the wine.

And every time they had bread or wine after that, they thought about Jesus.

Prayer
Help us, God, never to forget Jesus.

DAY THIRTY-FIVE

Who Jesus Prayed For

John 17:1–26

efore Jesus was arrested and taken away, he knelt under the moonlight in the Garden of Gethsemane and said a wonderful prayer that John, one of his disciples, wrote down.

Maybe you can guess who Jesus prayed for …

First, he prayed for himself, and asked God to be with him as he faced this scary time.

Next, he prayed for his disciples, and asked God to give them strength for the days ahead.

And after that, Jesus prayed for … US.

Jesus prayed that we would know how much he loves us and how we all belong in God's great family of love.

Jesus prayed a lot for this family that you and I are part of. More than anything else, he prayed that even though we may worship God in different ways and at different times, even though we might sometimes believe different things, Jesus prayed that we all might be ONE family.

One family kept together in love.

Prayer

Dear God, thank you that Jesus prayed for ME.
Help me to do my part in God's great family of love

DAY THIRTY-SIX

Jesus Dies

Luke 23:44–46

The world turned dark at three o'clock
The day that Jesus died.
The flowers trembling, hung their heads,
And God in heaven cried.

Prayer

God, in your mercy, hear our prayers.

DAY THIRTY-SEVEN

The Quiet Tomb

Matthew 28:57–66

fter Jesus died, Nicodemus and Joseph of Arimathea carefully took his body, wrapped it in a white cloth, and carried him to a quiet cave on the hillside. They put Jesus's body inside and sealed the entrance with a huge stone.

And all that quiet day … two Roman guards stood outside the tomb, keeping watch.

The disciples huddled together in Jerusalem, wondering what would happen next.

Mary Magdalene gathered spices and oils in her home so that she could go and anoint Jesus's body.

Jesus lay in the tomb.

God waited in heaven.

It was over.

Or was it?

Prayer

Thank you, God, for light in the darkness and hope in the hardest of times.
Help us to bring hope to those who need it this Lent.

DAY THIRTY-EIGHT

What Mary Saw

Mark 16:9–15

When Mary came back and peered in the cave,
Alone and scared, but terribly brave,
She saw Jesus there—could it really be true?
He'd come back to life, like he said he would do.

Can you imagine how Mary Magdalene felt in that hope-filled garden when she discovered that Jesus was alive? It must have been absolutely unbelievable! After that, Jesus appeared to his followers in a locked room, talked to two travelers on the road to Emmaus, and even made breakfast for his disciples on the beach.

Before Jesus went back to heaven, he told his followers to go out into all the world to tell others about him. As followers of Jesus, that includes us too. But sometimes, the very best way to tell others about Jesus is not through what we say, but what we *do*.

Let's love more this season. Let's look out for the lonely and the left out, let's help feed the hungry, let's be a friend to the friendless. If we do all those things, we'll be telling the world about Jesus and his wonderful way of love.

Prayer
Dear God, help us to take what we've learned this Lent into the world.
Show us how to spread the wonderful news of Jesus and his love however and wherever we can.

DAY THIRTY-NINE

Spread the Light

As we think about Lent and the stories we've heard,
Of whom Jesus was and the love that he shared,
Imagine God whisper:
"Now, go—spread the light.
Happy Lent to all and to all … a goodnight."

DAY FORTY

'Twas the Season of Lent

'Twas the season of Lent, when for forty whole days
God's people were trying to think of new ways
To be more like Jesus—to love, care, and give,
In hopes that they'd choose the right way to live.

On this journey through Lent, they were hoping to find
How to forgive, to pray, and be kind.
To think less of themselves, how to put others first,
To help heal the world of its sorrows and hurts.

But the story of Lent began long, long ago …
In a dry, dusty desert where no flowers grow.
For forty long days and forty long nights,
Jesus listened to God and chose what was right.

Then Jesus set out and found a good team
Of women and men who shared God's great dream.
And out on the hillside and by the lakeshore
His followers listened, eager for more.

He taught them to love, he taught them to pray,
He told them that God was with them each day.
And the calm in his voice, the words that he said,
Soon let listeners know—they had nothing to dread.

For those who were lonely, left out, or in pain,
It was Jesus who saw them and called them by name.
He brought hope to ALL with words that were true
To Martha and Mary and Zacchaeus too.

Whether young or old, or tiny or tall,
None of that mattered to Jesus at all.
Friend to the friendless, the sad or the scared,
Everyone loved the Good News Jesus shared.

But sometimes when Jesus lay down in his bed,
Visions of danger danced round in his head.
His enemies came and they took him away.
And soon, Jesus died on a dark, lonely day.

The cave where they laid him was sealed with a stone.
The disciples and Mary were left all alone.
They couldn't believe that they'd lost their good friend,
But his story's not over—it wasn't the end!

When Mary came back and peered in the cave,
Alone and scared, but terribly brave,
She saw Jesus there—could it really be true?
He'd come back to life, like he said he would do.

As we think about Lent and the stories we've heard,
Of whom Jesus was and the love that he shared,
Imagine God whisper:
"Now, go—spread the light.
Happy Lent to all and to all … a goodnight."